Girl in the Gold[

Winner of the 2004 Governor General's Literary Award for Drama

"A quirky cocktail consisting of equal parts Pinter, Orton, and Disney, shaken by author-director Morris Panych in his own distinctive style."—*Variety*

Vigil

Winner of the 1996 Jessie Richardson Award for Outstanding Play or Musical

"A small masterpiece."—*Globe and Mail*

What Lies Before Us

Short-listed for the 2007 Governor General's Literary Award for Drama

"Panych neatly balances existential questions with funny dialogue and pleasingly absurd characters."—*Canadian Literature*

Sextet

"*Sextet* is not just a wonderfully entertaining piece of theatre, it will make you think about love, sex, procreation, and music in ways you've never done before."—*Toronto Star*

The Shoplifters

Winner of the 2015 Edgerton Foundation New Play Award

"*The Shoplifters* is a gem in a minor key, as a work of literature and a play."—*Georgetowner*

The Trespassers

"With *The Trespassers*, Panych has crafted the theatrical equivalent of Johnny Cash's final output – a melancholic, darkly humourous, and wrenchingly beautiful portrait of life, death, love, and family."—*Waterloo Record*

WITHROW PARK

ALSO BY MORRIS PANYCH

*7 Stories**

*Benevolence**

The Cost of Living

*Earshot**

*The Ends of the Earth**

*The Dishwashers**

*Girl in the Goldfish Bowl**

*Gordon**

*In Absentia**

Last Call: A Post-Nuclear Cabaret

Life Science

*Laurence & Holloman**

Other Schools of Thought (including *Life Science, 2B WUT UR,*
    and *Cost of Living*)*

The Overcoat

*Sextet**

*The Shoplifters**

Still Laughing (including *The Government Inspector, Hotel
    Peccadillo,* and *The Amorous Adventures of Anatol*)*

The Story of a Sinking Man

*The Trespassers**

*What Lies Before Us**

*Vigil**

* Published by Talonbooks

WITHROW PARK

A Play

MORRIS PANYCH

Talonbooks

Talonbooks
9259 Shaughnessy Street, Vancouver, British Columbia, Canada V6P 6R4
talonbooks.com

Talonbooks is located on xʷməθkʷəy̓əm, Sḵwx̱wú7mesh, and səlilwətaɬ Lands.

First printing: 2024

Typeset in Minion
Printed and bound in Canada on 100% post-consumer recycled paper

Cover image by Ken MacDonald

Talonbooks acknowledges the financial support of the Canada Council for the Arts, the Government of Canada through the Canada Book Fund, and the Province of British Columbia through the British Columbia Arts Council and the Book Publishing Tax Credit.

Rights to produce *Withrow Park*, in whole or in part, in any medium by any group, amateur or professional, are retained by the author. Interested persons are requested to contact the author's agent: Pam Winter, Gary Goddard Agency, 250 The Esplanade, Suite 304, Toronto, ON, M5A 1J2; tel.: (416) 928-0299 x 1; email: pam@ggagency.ca; web: www.ggagency.ca.

Library and Archives Canada Cataloguing in Publication

Title: Withrow Park : a play / Morris Panych.
Names: Panych, Morris, author.
Identifiers: Canadiana 20240381718 | ISBN 9781772016208 (softcover)
Subjects: LCGFT: Drama.
Classification: LCC PS8581.A65 W58 2024 | DDC C812/.54—dc23

For Maureen MacDonald and all our departed friends who remind us how brief is this chance

1   Playwright's Note

3   Production History

4   Characters and Setting

5   Act One

65   Act Two

PLAYWRIGHT'S NOTE

Life is short and, for me, getting quite a bit shorter. As friends around me disappear into the vast beyond, I think of the "tempus fugit" of my failed Latin class days. "Present active indicative" (one of my favourite conjugations). Time flies! The horses' heads are towards eternity, yes, and the carriage will soon stop here. It's a bleak outlook from my front window as I wait, and yet a promising one. There are things still to be learned out there. Adventures to be had before the last to that undiscovered country.

It was my father who first introduced me to death. I was only six when he took me up in his arms, holding me over my grandmother's coffin so I could kiss her goodbye, and telling me she was "asleep forever," which sounded quite nice. The last time I saw him, he was taking his own eternal nap, and I was pushing the start button on the cremation furnace. Some time has passed since then: twenty years with maybe twenty more ahead. A friend remarked at the most recent memorial I attended, "It's our row, now." Yes, we're holding on to our numbers, listening nervously for them to be called here in this Service Ontario for the damned otherwise known as the senior years. In the meantime, what can we make of it, this brief postponement? While there's still time.

Earlier in my writing career, death was far away and happened to other people, a metaphor. I killed off characters with the stroke of a pen. Now that the ink is wet, waiting to scribble my name, I wonder if I should've been so callous. Closer to the end than the beginning, now, I feel like the punchline to my own morbid joke. But I deserve it. And I offer here, as an apology for my lifelong impertinence, reparation: because I could not stop for death, this play instead.

—MORRIS PANYCH

PRODUCTION HISTORY

Withrow Park was first produced in the Mainspace at the Tarragon Theatre in Toronto from November 7 to December 10, 2023, with the following cast and crew:

ARTHUR	Benedict Campbell
MARION	Corrine Koslo
JANET	Nancy Palk
SIMON	Johnathan Sousa

Director	Jackie Maxwell
Assistant Director	Bryn Kennedy
Set Designer	Ken MacDonald
Costume Designer	Joyce Padua
Lighting Designer	Kimberly Purtell
Sound Designer and Composer	Jacob Lin 林鴻恩
Stage Manager	Sandy Plunkett
Apprentice Stage Manager	Emily Cornelius

Thanks to Tarragon Theatre for nurturing and developing Canadian playwriting for over half a century.

CHARACTERS

MARION: A singular character, outspoken and contrary. Janet's sister and permanent houseguest. Sixties.

JANET: A practical woman with poor eyesight. Owner of the house. Arthur's ex-wife. Sixties.

SIMON: A handsome but dishevelled thirty-year-old man. His looks are distressed, rugged. He's unshaven, and the suit he's wearing is crumpled with a faded T-shirt underneath. He wears worn sneakers without socks. He could either be very trendy or not at all so.

ARTHUR: A not-unattractive but sad-looking man. In quite good physical shape but with the requisite bald patch. Janet's ex-husband. Sixties.

SETTING

A tall, Edwardian house with a large window overlooking a city park.

ACT ONE

Top: Corrine Koslo as Marion in Tarragon Theatre's production of *Withrow Park* by Morris Panych, November 2023

Bottom from left: Benedict Campbell as Arthur, Corrine Koslo as Marion, Johnathan Sousa as Simon, and Nancy Palk as Janet in Tarragon Theatre's production of *Withrow Park* by Morris Panych, November 2023

Photographs by Cylla von Tiedemann

SCENE ONE

*The front room of the house. At first there is blackness, then
a knock at the door. Lights up on MARION. She is reading
a book, a heavy and slightly outdated one. A second knock.
She looks up for a moment. Her older sister JANET enters
from the back.*

JANET
Why don't you answer it?

MARION
It's not my house.

*With a passing look of disdain, JANET goes off to the front
entry. Although we can't see who she's talking to, JANET is
greeted at the door by SIMON. The conversation between
them, either not visible or only partially so, is just loud
enough to be heard.*

JANET
(*offstage*) Hello.

SIMON
(*offstage*) Good morning.

Beat.

JANET
(*offstage*) Good morning.

SIMON
(*offstage*) I wanted to introduce myself.

JANET
(*offstage*) You're not selling anything, are you? Because we have
everything. I don't mean everything. We have everything we
need at the moment.

SIMON
(*offstage*) Do you?

JANET
(*offstage*) At the moment.

    Beat.

(*offstage*) Is there something I can help you with?

SIMON
(*offstage*) I'm new to the area. I just wanted to introduce myself.

JANET
(*offstage*) To the area. Oh.

    MARION tries to peer around the door into the vestibule
    from the safe distance of her chair.

SIMON
(*offstage*) My name is Simon. Simon Bodmer.

JANET
(*offstage*) Oh. Simon. I'm Janet. Wallace. Nice to meet you.

SIMON
(*offstage*) Very nice to meet you, Janet Wallace.

JANET
(*offstage*) Or just – Janet – would be – yes. And very nice to
meet you. Too.

SIMON
(*offstage*) So.

JANET
(*offstage*) Would you like to – come in?

SIMON
(*offstage*) Oh, no.

MARION
No.

JANET
(*offstage*) No?

SIMON
(*offstage*) No. I just wanted to introduce myself. I won't keep you, Janet. I'm on my way to an appointment. Just wanted to introduce myself.

JANET
(*offstage*) Well, it's awfully nice to meet you, Mr. Bodmer –

SIMON
(*offstage*) Simon, please. I'm in the neighbourhood.

JANET
(*offstage*) Well, please do drop by sometime when you have the time to – well, when you have the time – to drop by!

SIMON
(*offstage*) I will, thank you. Goodbye.

JANET
(*offstage*) Goodbye.

> With that the door closes and JANET returns to the living room with a bounce in her step.

JANET
Bodmer.

> MARION is waiting, not looking up from her book.

MARION
Is he handsome?

JANET
I didn't have my glasses.

MARION
You're wearing them.

JANET
(*realizing*) Oh dear.

MARION
They always are. That's how you know.

JANET
Know what?

MARION
Did he say what he wanted?

JANET
To introduce himself.

MARION
A likely story.

JANET
What?

MARION
Nothing. Just very odd.

JANET
Why is it odd?

MARION
We're not exactly the most conspicuous house around. Children don't even come here for Halloween.

JANET
Children don't come here for Halloween because you take your teeth out. I thought you were going somewhere this morning.

MARION
It's going to rain.

JANET
Have you never heard of an umbrella?

MARION
I have things I have to do first, so I thought if I do them in the meantime it might have already rained and then I can go out without having to carry an umbrella because I always lose them and, anyway, they're awkward in certain situations. Ask Arthur.

JANET's attention has drifted back out the window.

JANET
He was quite – oddly dressed, wrinkled suit. Or is that what people are wearing now? Why am I asking you?

MARION
You're not.

JANET
What situations?

MARION
Eh?

JANET
What situations are awkward with an umbrella?

MARION
Umbrella shopping, for one.

JANET
Why did I ask?

MARION
Have you ever tried it? They think you've stolen it. You go waltzing out of an umbrella store with your umbrella, they think you've stolen it. It happened to Arthur, only in his case he had stolen it, but only by accident.

MARION moves away from the window.

JANET
I'm going up to the unfriendly fish market. Do you want anything?

MARION
I'm good for fish, thanks.

JANET
Don't be funny. While I'm up there, do you want me to get you anything? I have to go to the unfriendly fish market and then I have my eye appointment. If you want anything, I'll pick it up.

MARION
The gin is low.

JANET
Good God. Really?

MARION
Don't look at me.

JANET
He's getting worse. Not that he doesn't deserve it, but do you think he might actually be in some sort of despair?

MARION
"Despair?" Are you reading *Madame Bovary* again?

JANET
I haven't read it in the first place. "Despair" is a word.

MARION
But is it "le mot juste?"

JANET
I'll get gin.

JANET goes to leave, but stops.

It is odd, but I like it. How many people these days take the trouble to drop by to introduce themselves?

MARION
Hardly dropping by.

JANET
I still don't know the name of the man next door, and he's lived there for four years.

MARION
Tom.

JANET
How do you know?

MARION
He introduced himself to me. Not so much introduced as corrected me when I called him something else, which is always the best way of finding things out. It's how I know he's not an accountant. What sort of fish are you getting?

JANET
Tilapia. I feel self-conscious now. Tom. He's never even said hello to me.

MARION
When did people start saying "tilapia" without any irony?

JANET
It's not a particularly ironic fish.

MARION

If you said "tilapia" without any irony a few years ago, people would have thought you were horribly pretentious. Now, people are saying it all over the place.

JANET sighs.

JANET

Would you prefer another species?

MARION

Basmati rice, there's another one. Nobody said "basmati rice," and now everyone does.

JANET

How is that book? The one in your lap that you're not reading.

MARION

Why would I read it when there's so much else going on?

JANET

You could've fooled me. I'm off.

MARION

Don't worry. He'll be back.

JANET

Who?

MARION

The shabbily dressed man at the door who said his name was Simon, which may or may not be true.

JANET

Why do you say that?

MARION

Because he wants something.

JANET
I mean, why would he make up a name?

MARION
I can't explain his motives.

JANET
And what makes you so sure he wants something?

MARION
(as if quoting) When you stop wanting something, you die.

JANET
Did somebody say that?

MARION
I did.

JANET
Well, whatever he wants, (brightly) I hope we have it.

*JANET leaves, closing the front door behind her. ARTHUR
enters in a housecoat.*

ARTHUR
What's all the commotion?

MARION
Nothing.

ARTHUR
Somebody at the door.

MARION
A handsome man in a rumpled suit. We can't go into details.
Janet has fallen instantly in love with him and gone off
to get fish.

ARTHUR
You're making that up.

    Beat.

Did anybody call?

MARION
If by "anybody" you mean a small-framed Filipino man who
dyes his hair a colour that is not the colour of human hair, the
answer is no. If by "call" you mean from a gas-station phone
booth somewhere in Arizona, weeping uncontrollably, and
asking your forgiveness for running off with someone younger
and more interesting than you, the answer is still no.

    Beat. ARTHUR goes to the window. He sighs heavily.

ARTHUR
What's happening in the park this morning?

MARION
Children are playing and dogs are being walked. It's a
whirlwind of social activity.

ARTHUR
Did she say anything?

MARION
About what?

ARTHUR
About anything?

MARION
What's there to say? It's an abomination.

    ARTHUR crosses back through the room, sighing as he exits.

ARTHUR
I suppose I'll have cornflakes.

ARTHUR exits.

SCENE TWO

Later. ARTHUR sits, reading a newspaper. JANET enters in pursuit of something she has instantly forgotten and leaves abruptly. ARTHUR takes no apparent notice of either her entrance or exit. But when she next returns, a few beats later, he senses her hovering.

ARTHUR
What time is it?

JANET
I don't know.

ARTHUR
Dining room.

JANET
What?

ARTHUR
Your other, better glasses are in the dining room.

JANET starts to exit.

ARTHUR
I think I'll turn in early. I'm exhausted.

JANET
What've you done all day?

ARTHUR
What did the eye doctor say?

JANET
Nothing.

ARTHUR
He can't have said nothing.

JANET
Not good news. Both eyes.

ARTHUR
Surgery?

JANET
A trabeculectomy; not for me. One should never have anything done to them that's more than five syllables.

ARTHUR
Yes, but –

JANET
(*quickly changing the subject*) Did you call him?

ARTHUR
I am not calling him. Anyway, he's in Palm Springs with a dog walker. Need we know more?

JANET
By the way, you're drinking too much.

ARTHUR
Define "too much."

JANET
If you're going to drink too much, you should drink wine.

ARTHUR
Why?

JANET
Because it's wine. People look at our recycling when they pass.

ARTHUR
  Who?

JANET
  People. Neighbours. They peruse the recycling. I've seen them.
  I'm looking at it from their perspective.

ARTHUR
  How do you know the neighbours aren't hiding their bottles
  under the newspapers? "Judge not lest ye be judged."

JANET
  I think it's in poor taste to quote the Bible in defence
  of alcoholism.

ARTHUR
  There's nothing left to do but drink.

JANET
  That can't be true.

ARTHUR
  So, tell me about this man.

JANET
  What man?

ARTHUR
  At the door. Oh my God, you're pretending you don't care.

JANET
  He was a very – pleasant person. And polite. New to the area.

ARTHUR
  Good-looking, she said.

JANET
  Not your type, Arthur.

ARTHUR
Janet –

JANET
Dinner is almost ready. It's fish.

ARTHUR
Not another one of your salmon experiments.

JANET
No. It's a bottom feeder with a high level of contaminants.

ARTHUR
Why would you make a dish no one likes?

JANET
Don't worry. I can't read the recipe anyway.

> *JANET exits. ARTHUR cries. He stops crying. He continues*
> *to read. MARION enters, taking her position, with book.*
> *ARTHUR moves to the window.*

MARION
I think a dog is the answer.

ARTHUR
What's the question?

MARION
If a person has a dog, then they don't think about
themselves anymore.

ARTHUR
There's a woman over there with a little whippet who talks on
the telephone –

MARION
The whippet?

ARTHUR

The woman. Have you seen her? By the fountain? The one with the impossibly short hair. She walks her dog to a bench by the water fountain and talks the whole time to some boyfriend on her phone. Never even looks at the poor creature.

MARION

How do you know it's a boyfriend?

ARTHUR

Posture. She leans into the phone with the other shoulder up. Like this. He's probably thinking, "How did I end up with this idiot?"

MARION

The boyfriend?

ARTHUR

The whippet. Well, the boyfriend too, no doubt, but I was thinking about the life of your average dog. While it may be true that we get the company we deserve, I don't think that's the case with animals. Anyway, my point is, having a dog will make you no less self-involved than you already are.

MARION

I wasn't thinking for me, I was thinking for you. I don't like dogs. Good heavens. I don't even like hot dogs.

ARTHUR

Then why do you want me to have one?

MARION

To keep you company in your old age.

ARTHUR

I'm not that old.

MARION

You will be.

ARTHUR
So will you.

MARION
I have my exit strategy.

ARTHUR
Yes, we've all heard your exit strategy. It won't work. In order to drive off a cliff, you have to be able to drive.

MARION
I have a general plan. What sort of plan have you got?

ARTHUR
You're not really serious about ending it all.

MARION
People drift towards oblivion. I find that my life has become more focused ever since I decided to end it.

ARTHUR
Have you set a date?

MARION
I've set a day, but not a year. I've decided it has to be my birthday.

ARTHUR
Isn't that coming up?

MARION
Probably too short notice for this year. I still have a few loose ends. There's a mystery I'm trying to solve.

ARTHUR
Oh?

MARION
That man who came by this morning.

ARTHUR

The handsome one in the rumpled suit?

MARION

He's up to something.

Unconvinced, ARTHUR continues reading.

I saw him a week ago, in the park, from my window, sitting in
the park, on a bench, all by himself, looking up at the house.
And I think he saw me.

ARTHUR

Are you making this up?

MARION

It was about three in the morning.

ARTHUR

Three in the morning? How do you know it was him?

MARION

I got up because I couldn't sleep. I had that dream again where
I have half an hour to catch a plane. I happened to look out
the window. There was a man, in the park, sitting looking right
up at the house. I wouldn't have known, it was only a shape,
could've been anything. Except that suddenly a car turned up
Logan and the headlights lit everything, the park, my window.
That's when he saw me. Then the car stopped, and the lights
went out, and two men got out. Drug deal? You tell me. They
didn't see me, but he did, clear as anything, standing in the
window. I think he might've smiled at me. And I knew, sooner
or later, he'd have to come by here, provided, of course, it wasn't
just a dream, which now I know it wasn't because now he's
turned up. Unless I'm still dreaming, which, according to
what's-his-name, that Spanish writer, is entirely possible. Or was
he South American?

ARTHUR
It's possible to be both.

MARION
Or neither.

ARTHUR
How could he be looking at you if he didn't even see you?

MARION
He did see me. I'm a witness to something. If I only knew what.

ARTHUR
But before the headlights. What was he looking at if you were completely in the dark?

MARION
Calderón! How did I remember that?

ARTHUR
With any luck you'll forget it again.

ARTHUR leaves. Blackout.

SCENE THREE

Later in the week, an afternoon discussion. JANET,
MARION, and ARTHUR, from various positions in the room,
peer out the window as they drink tea.

JANET
  Maybe we should just go over there and talk to him.

MARION
  Are you insane?

JANET
  Why not? He just came over here.

ARTHUR
  Is he still there? He's still there.

MARION
  Just swinging on the swing. What does that mean, I wonder?

JANET
  He knows we're watching him.

ARTHUR
  Our lives could be in danger.

JANET
  Well, the best way to ensure our collective safety is to let him
  know that we're all in on it.

MARION
  I agree.

ARTHUR
  With what?

MARION
If we're together – he's not going to get rid of us all. That would be an awful lot of logistical work. There's only so much you can do with three bodies.

ARTHUR
There's always the garden.

JANET
He's not a psychopath.

MARION
Are you sure?

JANET
We should have him over for dinner and find out.

MARION
Janet's right. He didn't murder her when she answered the door.

ARTHUR
You let her answer the door thinking she'd be murdered?

MARION
Afternoon is not the time.

JANET
This whole thing is ridiculous. Remember the headless man you saw in that truck that turned out to be a coat on the back of a seat?

MARION
I was having a nervous breakdown at the time.

JANET
I'll tell you what this is: it's the sad, undeniable fact that none of us has anything better to do with our time. A man sits in the park –

MARION
Every day for two weeks.

JANET
He's watching us, yes, because every time he looks up, we're watching him. Maybe he likes the park. Maybe he just wants to sit there and swing back and forth all by himself. Maybe he's no one, doing nothing. Just like us. I wish he did want to murder us.

JANET exits.

ARTHUR
Is it too early to start drinking?

MARION
She's always been such a killjoy.

ARTHUR
It's true that we have too much time on our hands.

MARION
I'll go over there myself. I'll confront him directly.

ARTHUR
Why did I retire? What was I thinking? That was the beginning of the end.

MARION
If he kills me, he kills me. I'll be quite happy to be dead.

ARTHUR
I shouldn't have come out. Ever.

MARION
No, you shouldn't have. It ruined her life and did you no good whatsoever. That's two lives destroyed out of some mistaken principle of self-realization.

ARTHUR
Thank you for that.

MARION
He's taking a drink from the fountain now. Clearly he has no gastric concerns.

ARTHUR
And it wasn't a "principle of self-realization."

MARION
What was it, then? You were perfectly happy your whole life and then suddenly – three months ago. Janet lived for you. *Now* what does she have to live for?

ARTHUR
As I recall, you were the catalyst for my coming out.

MARION
How?

ARTHUR
I believe you told her I was gay.

MARION
That was speculation. I didn't imagine in a million years it was anywhere near the truth. Well yes, I did.

ARTHUR
It's too late now.

MARION
Off he goes. Where to now, I wonder.

ARTHUR
Too late.

MARION
Is it? Arthur, what do we live for? Let me put the question to you another way.

ARTHUR
Oh, it's a question.

MARION
Why do we bother?

ARTHUR
I don't know, but I'm sure you'll answer it for me.

MARION
Let me answer it for you. We live for nothing. There is no reason, except to take up space. Your reason could be Janet if you think about it for half a second. You could forget this impulsive whimsy of yours. Besides, you're too old for it. There's your blood pressure to think of.

ARTHUR
Not impulsive. And yes, I'm too old, but am I?

MARION
Your weird little pediatrician has run off with somebody else, and you're left empty-handed. I never liked him.

ARTHUR
You've never met him.

MARION
At the farmer's market, by the zucchini blossoms. He was wearing a dress.

ARTHUR
That's not a dress. It's a tunic.

MARION
You need to get back into a closet, Arthur. And not his.

ARTHUR
I don't know if you're aware of the conventions, but once you come out, you can't go back in again.

MARION
Why not? Sir John A. Macdonald did.

ARTHUR
Did he?

MARION
Didn't he?

MARION walks away from the window. ARTHUR looks out.

ARTHUR
Look at that sad creature.

MARION
The man?

ARTHUR
No, that whippet. He just wants to go hang out with other dogs, but no. He's stuck with some woman on a phone.

MARION
How do you know what he wants?

MARION takes up her book.

ARTHUR
It's what every dog wants.

MARION
It's better if you can't do something you want. Gives you something to long for. I bet he's perfectly happy wishing he could run free but not doing it. And anyway, he doesn't look very intelligent. He'd run right into a car.

ARTHUR
Right into a car.

A mantle clock rings five times.

ARTHUR
It's Janet. Look. She's over there. She's – (*suddenly alarmed*) talking to him.

MARION
The whippet?

ARTHUR
The man.

Blackout.

SCENE FOUR

*A few days later. Afternoon. SIMON, about whom so much
has been speculated, now stands looking out the window.
In a moment, ARTHUR rounds the corner, speaking
as he enters.*

ARTHUR
You know, Janet, I've been thinking –

ARTHUR stops, seeing SIMON.

Hello.

SIMON
Hello. I'm Simon. Simon Bodmer.

ARTHUR
Oh, yes. Yes! Oh! Of course! Yes! The man in the park. I mean,
at the door.

SIMON
Sorry?

ARTHUR
You – came to introduce yourself the other day. Came to the
door, to – introduce yourself.

SIMON
I did.

ARTHUR
New to the neighbourhood.

SIMON
To the neighbourhood, yes.

ARTHUR
Welcome. Where is – uh – ?

SIMON
Janet?

ARTHUR
Oh, we're using first names. That's –

SIMON
She's making me some tea.

ARTHUR
Tea?

SIMON
You have a wonderful view from here.

ARTHUR
View?

SIMON
Of the park. You can see practically the whole park from here.

ARTHUR
Practically. But not – so well at night.

SIMON
No?

ARTHUR
Well, there isn't a lot of light in the park, at night. Almost none.
So – things are going on, but you don't, often, necessarily see
them. Not at three in the morning. Or four.

SIMON
What sorts of things?

ARTHUR
What?

SIMON
What sorts of things are going on?

ARTHUR
Well, you wouldn't know because you can't necessarily see
them. It's night. It's dark. It's three in the morning. Or four.
People sitting there. Looking at you. You wouldn't know. It's the
middle of the night. And anyway, you're asleep. Some of you.

SIMON
You mean people hang out in the park.

ARTHUR
I –

Beat.

SIMON
Are you a relative of –

ARTHUR
Sorry?

SIMON
How do you know Janet?

ARTHUR
I'm Arthur. I'm her ex-husband. So related but – in litigation.
I'm kidding, that's a joke. We're sorting things out.

SIMON
Oh, so you don't live here.

ARTHUR
No, I do live here.

SIMON
Interesting dichotomy. A categorical variable but luckily not a polytomous one, I'm kidding it's a joke. And living is sometimes figurative, isn't it?

ARTHUR
Is it?

SIMON
Arthur. Of legend.

ARTHUR
Not much of a legend. I – moved out for a couple of months but that didn't – work out terribly well, so I moved back in again. I don't – really like living by myself. I wasn't – wasn't actually living by myself, but then – I found that I was.

Suddenly, from ARTHUR, a cry that he quickly gets hold of.

SIMON
This is an emotional time, I see.

ARTHUR
So. How long have you been here?

SIMON
Ten minutes.

ARTHUR
I mean … in the neighbourhood.

SIMON
Not long. It's a nice neighbourhood; I really like it here. The people are very friendly – ready with a smile.

ARTHUR
They are?

SIMON
If you smile pre-emptively, it's always disarming. Like tossing a
bomb, but a nice one. One that explodes with happiness. How
long have you lived here?

ARTHUR
We moved here about twenty-five years ago. It was my mother's
house. She lived with us, here, until she – she – sadly –

SIMON
Passed away?

ARTHUR
Went insane, actually. They called it paranoid personality
disorder, but – they had to call it something. One day when
we weren't at home she took all the furniture in the house and
dragged it down into the cellar. I can't even remember her
explanation. Well, it was insane, of course. It's amazing how
mad a person can become without anybody even realizing it.

SIMON
Even themselves.

ARTHUR
Especially themselves. One day she's watching game shows, the
next day she's cowering under an armoire in the basement with
a large amount of Boston lettuce in her possession. Sometimes
I think I'm headed in the same direction. Not the game shows,
but as the years go by the furniture-in-the-cellar scenario makes
more and more sense, as does the lettuce.

An awkward beat.

ARTHUR
I wonder where that tea is.

On cue, JANET enters with a tray of tea things.

JANET
Oh, hello. You've met Mr. Bodmer, I see.

ARTHUR
Yes.

SIMON
He was telling me about his mother.

JANET
Really? Why?

ARTHUR
The subject came up.

JANET
What subject is that?

ARTHUR
I wonder if I could have a word with you?

JANET
Well, not now, Arthur. I'm having tea with Mr. Bodmer.

SIMON
Please call me Simon.

JANET
Would you like some tea? Arthur?

ARTHUR
I –

Standing behind SIMON, ARTHUR grimaces.

JANET
Why are you making that face?

SIMON turns to him, ARTHUR now with no expression.

ARTHUR
I'm not making a face.

JANET
Yes, you are.

ARTHUR
I am not making a face. Mr. Bodmer was just telling me he's new
to the neighbourhood.

JANET
We all know that.

ARTHUR
I've never met him.

JANET
I told you the other day. He came by to introduce himself. I told
you. And now you're acting as if you didn't know and making
strange grimacing faces.

ARTHUR
My wife doesn't know the difference, apparently, between
smiling simply and unaffectedly and grimacing. I was smiling
simply and unaffectedly, and she seems to have taken it as
making a face.

JANET
Nonsense. You were making a face because you think Mr.
Bodmer is a psychopath. (*turning her attention back to SIMON*)
They think you're a psychopath. He and my sister. It might be
your neighbourliness. Most people on this street don't speak
to one another, so naturally suspicion falls heavily on anyone
with any charm or personality. Don't worry, my sister thinks
everybody is a psychopath; and Arthur, of course, is a person
who just goes along with the prevailing trend.

SIMON
But how do I know *you're* not a psychopath, Arthur?

A strange beat.

You see the fun we can have?

ARTHUR
Janet, this is preposterous. Why are you telling Mr. Bodmer – ?
It was a joke, Mr. Bodmer.

SIMON
Simon –

ARTHUR
It was a joke. And I do not go along with the prevailing trend.

JANET
Ex-wife.

ARTHUR
What?

JANET
You called me your wife.

ARTHUR
We were married.

JANET
And now we're not. Arthur is gay, Simon. A very recent
development. Before that he was just emotionally unavailable.

SIMON
I see.

ARTHUR
I was a lot of things, Janet, but I was not emotionally
unavailable.

JANET
He was emotionally unavailable. Milk?

SIMON
Thank you.

JANET
We lived together, I suppose, by default. I suppose, when I think about it, Arthur was simply passing the time, like a fellow traveller you might meet in an airport terminal who is quite willing to share with you sometimes the most intimate details of their life with the understanding that at some point you will both go your separate ways and never see each other again, except that in Arthur's case he didn't go away.

ARTHUR
Why should I go away? I live here.

JANET
Did you say you were having tea, Arthur, or not having tea?

ARTHUR
Tea. Please.

SIMON
Excellent.

ARTHUR sits as JANET pours. Blackout.

SCENE FIVE

ARTHUR sits, looking out the window.

JANET
He'll be here any minute.

ARTHUR
It's decided. I'm going to leave.

JANET
When?

ARTHUR
You can't just say "when?" in that flat, off-handed tone. This is my house.

JANET
Our house. And you can't say "it's decided," as if there was a committee working away diligently on the question. You're not going anywhere. You never will.

ARTHUR
I think we should sell the house.

JANET
Why?

ARTHUR
I'll need the money to buy an apartment.

JANET
Can you not rent an apartment?

ARTHUR
Why should I be stuck in a rented apartment while you live here?

JANET
You can continue living here.

ARTHUR
I see. I can continue living here. You're giving me
your permission.

JANET
I'm not giving you my permission. It's a suggestion.

ARTHUR
Not much of a suggestion. I'm already living here.

JANET
Is this one of these circuitous conversations that ends in a
pointless argument? I have an idea. Why don't we dispense with
circuitousness and get right to the argument. In fact, let's avoid
the argument, too, while we're at it, and fast forward straight
to the end. You're a *stupid fucking idiot*; the end. Out I go, door
slam, scene. How's that?

ARTHUR
I don't know what's going on here.

JANET
I wish you would dress for dinner. Mr. Bodmer will be
here any minute.

ARTHUR
What's wrong with what I have on? Did you see
what *he* had on?

JANET
In a moral universe where there is no centre, and in a time
of equivalency and shifting values, there are very few things
governing our lives, Arthur. But underwear at dinner is where I
must draw the line.

ARTHUR
It's a T-shirt.

JANET
On a twenty-year-old, it's a T-shirt. On you, it's underwear.

ARTHUR
He wears one, and a suit that looks like somebody used it to
clean a grease trap.

JANET
What is this? Are you making a point? If you are, please let me
know so I can announce it at dinner, otherwise the point will
be lost on everyone, and you'll only end up looking like a man
who has no shirts to his name. Or worse, a sixty-six-year-old,
suddenly gay, retired schoolteacher who cannot face the truth
about himself.

ARTHUR
I have faced the truth about myself, which is why I'm retired,
why I'm gay, and not suddenly, and why I'm wearing a T-shirt.
Because the truth is, when you're sixty-six, you can do whatever
the fuck you want.

JANET
Is that why you became a homosexual?

ARTHUR
Janet, I did not become a homosexual. Now you're just trying
to provoke me.

JANET
I do wish you'd let me know twenty-five years ago, before I
moved in with you and your crazy mother.

ARTHUR
Why are you bringing this up? Why are you always
bringing this up?

JANET

Yes. Imagine if you'd just gone and put on a proper shirt.
This conversation wouldn't be happening. But instead,
you're sitting there in your underwear, having to defend your
impromptu sexuality.

ARTHUR

I'm not defending anything. It's not a position. It's who I am.

JANET

You have no idea who you are; you never have. You've admitted
it yourself. For example: you hated teaching and yet you did it
for forty-three years.

ARTHUR

I didn't hate teaching. I hated children.

JANET

And why have you become a vegetarian?

ARTHUR

Have I?

JANET

I don't know. Marion says you have.

ARTHUR

I eat fish. I eat chicken sometimes unless it's in curry.

JANET

You're trying on all these new things – none of which suit you,
by the way – one week you're a vegetarian who eats fish and
sometimes chicken, one week you're doing ceramics, badly, one
week you're studying, of all languages, Tágalog –

ARTHUR

(*correcting her pronunciation*) Tagálog –

JANET

And you wonder why I should question your sexual self-discovery. Not that it makes any difference whatsoever.

ARTHUR

Then why do you care?

JANET

(*suddenly, violently*) Because you broke my heart, Arthur! Completely and utterly.

Beat.

ARTHUR

You never said that before.

JANET

Why would I need to say it? Wasn't it obvious?

ARTHUR

You've been carrying on just fine. It's been three months.

JANET

Oh, Arthur, you really are a stupid fucking idiot.

JANET exits but quickly re-enters.

JANET

And to top it off, it was all for nothing. The man you were supposedly in love with is in Palm Springs with a dog walker.

ARTHUR

I wasn't "supposedly" in love with him. I *was* in love with him. I still *am* in love with him.

JANET

If I can't be your wife, can I at least be your friend? Here's some friendly advice: don't make yourself pathetic by continuing to be in love with somebody who no longer loves you.

ARTHUR
How do you just stop loving someone?

JANET
I did.

> *The doorbell rings and JANET goes to the door. MARION suddenly appears from the hallway.*

MARION
She's right, you know.

ARTHUR
What?

SIMON
(*offstage*) Hello.

MARION
You have made yourself pathetic.

JANET
(*offstage*) Hello.

ARTHUR
She stopped loving me? When?

JANET
(*offstage*) Come in!

MARION
Just now.

> *SIMON appears with JANET in the entryway, both smiling. Blackout.*

SCENE SIX

Following dinner, JANET, MARION, ARTHUR, and
SIMON enter the living room. SIMON has just told a very
funny story and they are all laughing and bursting with
admiration and appreciation for his amazing charm and
wit, and of course they've all been drinking.

JANET
  That is very funny. Very funny.

MARION
  Very funny.

ARTHUR
  Very.

MARION
  Were you always such a wit?

SIMON
  Just mentally ill.

  They all laugh.

JANET
  Join the club.

MARION
  What is "Bodmer"? Is that an alias?

JANET
  Why would he make up a name?

SIMON
  It's Swiss.

MARION

What other passports do you carry?

JANET

Marion.

SIMON

I'm a citizen of the world!

JANET

Didn't you say you lived in Ottawa? He already said that,
Marion. At dinner. He said he went to Carleton. He said he
studied psychology.

SIMON

It was one of my subjects, yes.

MARION

I mustn't have been paying attention.

JANET

She never does.

MARION

Unless it's something I'm not supposed to. Whenever I watch
the news on TV, I always look at their facial hair or the way
they tie their ties or how their hair is combed, but I have no
idea whatsoever what's going on in the world. The truth is, the
tie and the hair, to me, are what's really going on in the world.
Wouldn't you agree? It's the little secret details I like. The things
nobody else looks at. Whenever I go to the movies, I always
watch the audience. Much more interesting.

SIMON

You're perverse, is that it?

JANET

She's always been that way.

MARION

And my sister has always been the opposite. We could be
looking at the exact same thing and see something completely
different. Remember that woman a few years back, on the news,
who said her car went into the river, and she couldn't rescue her
children, and they drowned. Janet felt so sorry for her – do you
remember, Janet? – she saw the poor despairing victim, but I
wasn't listening to a word of it.

JANET

My goodness you're speaking loudly.

MARION

No. I was looking at her hair. I said, "Look at her hair, Janet.
She's just lost her two children, and she's crying into the camera
and telling this sad story, and it's all very tragic, but she's done
her hair." You have to ask what kind of mother would do their
hair in that situation? Turns out I was right. She murdered
them. In cold blood.

JANET

A real sleuth is our Marion.

MARION

Somebody has to be on the lookout in this neighbourhood.

SIMON

Not a lot of crime around here, I don't imagine.

MARION

Not so far.

JANET

Would you like some dessert, Simon?

MARION

Where did you live before you moved to this neighbourhood?

SIMON
    Where?

MARION
    In a halfway house?

SIMON
    I'd love some dessert, thank you. I was in residence. At Carleton.

MARION
    I forget. Is that maximum security or medium?

JANET
    It's a university. In Ottawa.

SIMON
    Before that I lived in Montréal. Laval to be exact.

MARION
    I don't know that institution.

SIMON
    And then Carleton, and after that I moved to Milton!

JANET
    You poor soul.

SIMON
    But I didn't stay long.

MARION
    No.

ARTHUR
    (*exclaiming suddenly*) Do you have the feeling I'm sitting here
    in my underwear?

SIMON
    Sorry?

ARTHUR
Do I appear to you, Simon, to be sitting here in my undershirt?

JANET
Oh Arthur, shut up.

ARTHUR
Why should I shut up? I'm having a conversation with our guest.

JANET
You're just embarrassing him. It won't be a conversation, it'll be a weird diatribe.

MARION
Arthur was a schoolteacher. They tend to be monologists.

ARTHUR
Am I embarrassing you, Simon?

SIMON
No, not at all. This is very nice cutlery.

JANET
It's his mother's.

ARTHUR
I'm not embarrassing him. Not at all.

MARION
He's going through one of those life changes. He hit his mid-sixties, retired, and went bonkers.

ARTHUR
I didn't go bonkers. But I did go on a journey.

SIMON
I've been on those.

JANET
Please tell us about yours, Simon.

ARTHUR
It was a trip to Machu Picchu.

SIMON
Oh.

JANET
Do you have to tell this story?

MARION
It'll be incredibly embarrassing.

JANET
Arthur, please.

ARTHUR
My wife booked the holiday.

JANET
Ex-wife.

ARTHUR
She thought it would be a good idea, as my retirement present, for us to go to Machu Picchu. Of all places.

JANET
You make it sound like forced exile.

ARTHUR
It was forced exile. I didn't want to go. In fact, I said to my darling ex-wife that I, specifically, didn't want to go to Machu Picchu, but she went ahead and booked it anyway. I have no interest in the Incas, Simon; none. But, you see, Janet has an interest in the Incas, God knows why, probably because they occupied cold, remote regions. High, unreachable plateaux.

JANET
Who wants coffee?

MARION
I'll have some.

JANET
Not a good idea. Simon?

SIMON
Yes, thanks.

JANET exits to the kitchen.

ARTHUR
It wasn't really a journey of true self-discovery until we actually got to Machu Picchu. You see, the whole way I kept trying to convince myself that this was what I passionately wanted, because, you see, it was what my wife, my ex-wife, told me I passionately wanted. "You want to stand high above the clouds, feeling a connection with an ancient people." Oh. Do I? Well. Then. And it wasn't until I had climbed those heights I never cared to climb and stood high above the clouds, looking down into valleys I couldn't care less about that I realized: this isn't who I am. Who I am is down there, somewhere. I have no idea who this is standing here, wearing an alpaca chullo with earflaps. Why else would I feel so disconnected to everything?

JANET returns with a tray and two coffees, cream, and sugar.

My wife has controlled my whole life, Simon. I always suspected but never quite understood the extent of it. Standing two miles up above the world, I suddenly felt how truly pointless my life was.

MARION
Lack of oxygen.

ARTHUR
Would you like to see some pictures?

SIMON
Love to.

ARTHUR exits.

MARION
Monologist. Told you.

SIMON
I loved Peru. I went there as a young man.

MARION
And here I thought *Colombia* was where all drugs came from.

JANET
Marion.

MARION
I tried to go to Machu Picchu once. I just ended up in a morgue.
That's a story.

JANET
Please don't tell it.

ARTHUR
(*offstage*) It wasn't a morgue. It was a funeral home.

MARION
I got into what I thought was an airport taxi, but it turned out
to be a hearse.

JANET
It wasn't a hearse.

MARION
I don't know what it was. It was a black car that looked like my airport taxi, and I ended up at a funeral. But here's the odd bit: her name was Marion – the victim, or whatever you call the dead person at a funeral.

JANET
The dead person.

MARION
Marion was her name, same as mine, so I had to stay. It was as if I had landed smack dab in the middle of my own memorial service. How I wept. But there was something cleansing about it. Truly cleansing. After that day, I embraced death wholly. I've been planning my demise ever since. Who could go to Central America after that?

JANET
Machu Picchu is in South America.

MARION
If you've never been there, what difference does it make? People talk about valleys on Mars. But are they really valleys if nobody has ever walked them?

JANET
Yes.

MARION
Janet is so pragmatic. She used to swallow money as a child.

JANET
What's that got to do with anything?

MARION
I think it formed your character.

ARTHUR returns, brandishing a photo album.

ARTHUR
Here we are. Pictures of our lives.

MARION
I have no pictures of myself because I refuse to have them taken.
I don't want anybody to remember me when I'm gone.

JANET
There's little worry of that.

MARION
I won't even have a funeral because I feel I've already had one.

JANET
What if we decide to have a funeral? A great big, bloated affair.
With a brass band and gospel choir.

MARION
You can't. It's my last request as of now. No fuss. There, I've said
it. You're all witnesses.

JANET
But you'll be dead and quite unable to stop us. I might decide
to dedicate a bench to you in the park. "In memory of Marion
Wallace, who loved this park so very much and spent many
thoughtful hours here thinking up ways to disrupt the lives of
others until mercifully she ended her own."

MARION
That's a lot to fit on one bench.

JANET
We'll make it a long bench.

ARTHUR sits close to SIMON.

ARTHUR
This was taken in Lima, on the way. The serape was Janet's idea,
of course. She used to dress me.

JANET
I did not.

MARION
I forget. Were you gay at that point and didn't know it,
or pretending to be straight?

ARTHUR
The shorts were not my idea either.

MARION
I was very lucky not to have married Arthur.

JANET
Oh, good heavens.

MARION
It was me he was initially interested in. But I turned him down.

ARTHUR
I wasn't interested in you at all.

MARION
We went out on three dates.

ARTHUR
The worst three dates of my life.

MARION
How can you say that? What about your first date with Janet?
His first date with Janet, they went to the shoe museum. How
did you not know he was gay at that point, I wonder? Imagine
taking your date to the shoe museum.

ARTHUR
I like shoes.

JANET
Why aren't you wearing any?

ARTHUR
It's my house. I can wear what I like, I can *not* wear what I like.

ARTHUR boldly removes his T-shirt.

There. See?

JANET
Splendid.

MARION
Have you shaved your chest?

SIMON
You don't need to remove your clothes on my account, Arthur.
(*returning to the album*) This looks like Cusco.

ARTHUR
Does it? My wife could tell you.

JANET
Put that back on. We're in the middle of dessert.

ARTHUR
(*to Simon*) We travelled for two weeks in the Andes, and I
never once looked up. (*to Janet*) I'm putting it back on, but not
because you said so.

JANET
Fine.

ARTHUR
It happens to be cold in here.

MARION
Janet likes to keep the temperature as cold as
humanly endurable.

SIMON
I find it perfectly comfortable.

MARION
Compared to where you've been.

SIMON
Exactly.

ARTHUR
There are no pictures after that. Not one single picture has been taken of anyone since that trip.

MARION
How does one decide to go into the drug-trafficking business? It can't just be for the money.

ARTHUR
That's Lima. What a despicable town.

MARION
You still haven't told us what you do.

ARTHUR
He studied psychology.

MARION
That doesn't mean anything. I studied Spanish and I can't even make a paella. I meant, what is it you do now that you've served your time, Simon?

SIMON
I'm still serving it. We all are. All of us, waiting in line.

MARION
For?

SIMON
What comes next.

A beat of reflection quickly punctured.

MARION
Meanwhile, have you found employment?

JANET
Marion will snooker you into it, so you might as well tell us.

MARION
I think it's more fun guessing.

SIMON
All right, why don't you guess?

MARION
How many guesses do we get?

SIMON
One.

MARION
Not much of a game.

JANET
Doctor.

MARION
Ignore her. You can't just throw out a guess without consulting us first.

ARTHUR
Especially if we have only one guess.

SIMON
How did you guess I was a doctor?

JANET
Because you look at us all in a very inquisitive way.
As if you're trying to understand the mechanics of us.
Does that make sense?

MARION
No.

ARTHUR
No.

SIMON
Yes.

JANET
And you said you studied psychology.

SIMON
I've studied many things. I'm still studying them.

JANET
We could use a psychologist around here.

SIMON
A lifting of your hearts is all you need.

ARTHUR
Oh, is that all!

SIMON
Arthur, you're trying to deal with an important realization
which has come rather late in your life.

MARION
Much too late.

SIMON
But perhaps not the realization you think. Janet, you're losing
your vision.

JANET
    How did you know that?

SIMON
    But in time –

JANET
    How did he know that?

SIMON
    You'll see things you couldn't have seen. Marion, you've decided
    to end your life, which is truly the beginning of it.

ARTHUR
    You know a lot about us for someone who knows
    nothing about us.

SIMON
    Yes. And now let me reveal a little something about myself,
    a story. Unfortunately, you won't remember any of it, because
    once I've told it, I will hypnotize all of you, causing you to
    forget everything I've said.

        A nervous laugh from the three hosts.

SIMON
    But the room will remember it.

JANET
    The room can't even remember where my glasses are.

SIMON
    You won't need them.

MARION
    Why are you going to hypnotize us?

SIMON
    Obviously because I don't want you to remember the story.

ARTHUR
Why not?

MARION
Does it involve homicide?

JANET
Marion –

SIMON
In a manner of speaking.

MARION
I knew it. I wasn't dreaming.

SIMON
No, you weren't.

MARION
Did you kill someone?

SIMON
No.

JANET
Marion –

SIMON
Someone killed me.

   Blackout.

ACT TWO

Top from left: Johnathan Sousa as Simon, with Benedict Campbell as Arthur, Corrine Koslo as Marion, and Nancy Palk as Janet in Tarragon Theatre's production of *Withrow Park* by Morris Panych, November 2023

Bottom: Nancy Palk as Janet in Tarragon Theatre's production of *Withrow Park* by Morris Panych, November 2023

Photographs by Cylla von Tiedemann

SCENE ONE

SIMON steps forward into light. He is talking to his hosts but facing the audience; JANET, MARION, and ARTHUR are seated as before but in a state of suspension.

SIMON

From this end of the park, you can look southwest and see the constellation Orion. In this direction, a million years of life await you, but how to get there? You can't just climb onto that swing and swing your way up and over the rooftops. To get there, you must learn the whole way, and you must learn, as well, the answers that will be asked of you when you arrive or be devoured by Ammit in the Hall of Two Truths. When your heart is weighed, it must be as light as a feather.

Yes, someone murdered me, stabbed me to death. Don't worry. I can't die, as you can see. And it's also quite possible I'm making all this up. If there are two truths, then this may be only one of them. Call it delusional or call it what you will. People have a hard time believing. It wasn't always the case. But here, in this time, inside these lovely homes, surrounding this pleasant green space, the truth must be made evident, must be seen to be believed. Any questions so far?

Silence. SIMON continues.

My spirit inhabited this person you see here, this corpse standing before you, this homeless man named Bodmer. I don't know where I came from. I had long forgotten. Alcohol and disease – or perhaps from Milton, or Laval. Who knows? I occupied this mind and sought harbour in this body. But not for long. I was found sleeping on a bench that night by some young men passing by in a car. Perhaps they were a little too drunk. They didn't expect a fight in return. And they certainly didn't expect to see a knife. But I kept one with me for situations like this. I would've been safer on the street of course – by some sewer grate, in an open area, but I came to love this park and

the people who live around it on these quiet, lovely streets. But I
have also seen their refuse. All that's tossed away. It had to come
to an end. I simply knew too much about them. The spirit of life
has been lost here. Instead, this accumulation of things, only to
be discarded. And yet there is something about you - the three
of you here, a longing to consume not things, but things that
are not things. I saw you look out from inside your window that
night, and I knew in an instant that you were looking for more,
for guidance upward. How to reach out from this place and
touch the stars. You know at least this one truth, now. It's not
enough to have lived your lives. There is more. Believe or don't
believe - it doesn't matter. The stars are waiting, regardless. And
time has found you here, hiding in plain sight.

    Beat.

The dessert was very nice but a little sweet.

    SIMON shows some knives and forks.

I also took some cutlery, thank you.

    *SIMON exits into the hallway and slams the front door,
    causing JANET, MARION, and ARTHUR to wake from
    their trance.*

SCENE TWO

MARION is seated, as in the first scene, reading. JANET enters, looking out the window. Her tone with MARION is harder, more resolute.

JANET
I'm off to get fish.

MARION
I thought you had an ophthalmologist appointment.

JANET
Yes. Death by a thousand eye drops.

MARION
We're out of gin.

JANET
Why doesn't she ever talk to whoever it is she's talking to in person?

MARION
Who?

JANET
The woman with the whippet. Will we ever see the other side of this conversation?

MARION
Fish? Aren't you making what I asked for?

JANET
If you want "kidneys Pamplona," you can cook them yourself.

MARION
It's my birthday. Quite possibly the last.

JANET

I am not eating anything that's had urine pass through it.

MARION

You're thinking of the bladder. Nobody eats bladder.
Not knowingly.

JANET

We're having empanada-style Sri Lankan fish patties with
curry aioli because that's what you asked for, for your birthday,
before you got it into your head that you had to eat the insides
of a lamb. By the way, there's silverware missing. Does it have
anything to do with you?

MARION

I wish it did.

JANET

I thought this wasn't your final year; besides, we have tickets to
the symphony next month, and if you commit suicide I'll have
to go with Arthur.

MARION

Why?

JANET

Because. Married, not married, it's all the same and always will
be. Our little lives uninterrupted.

MARION

Maybe not forever.

JANET

Don't you think it was strange that Mr. Bodmer never came for
dinner the other night?

MARION

No surprise.

JANET
Arthur must've scared him off when he came for tea, acting like
an idiot, making those faces.

*JANET speaks with sudden energy - turning back
into the room.*

I can't do this. I won't. Marion, I'm going somewhere. And
not to the ophthalmologists. I'm going to sell this house and
go somewhere.

MARION
When?

JANET
(*picking up velocity*) I'm retired, I have no commitments.
I could live in Mexico for a while. I could live quite simply in
some little place by the ocean. I could swim and write and cook.

MARION
You'd be all alone.

JANET
I like being alone. I don't know if I like being alone. I've
never been alone.

MARION
What about me?

JANET
Besides, I'll meet people. What about you?

MARION
Where will I go?

JANET
You're an adult, Marion. You can go wherever you like.

MARION
Then I'm coming with you.

JANET
I'm hardly getting away from my life if my life follows me there.

MARION
But your life does follow you.

JANET
Not if I reinvent myself.

MARION
Don't reinvent yourself. Not on my birthday.

JANET
I'm getting out of here. It's decided.

A spark has been lit.

JANET exits definitively. MARION closes her book.

MARION
Nobody gets out.

Blackout.

SCENE THREE

ARTHUR and JANET enter the house through the front entry, taking off coats and making their way into the living room. ARTHUR looks out the window as JANET sits, staring blankly. There is a long, considered silence, during which the room is still, as though the air itself couldn't move.

ARTHUR
God, I hate squirrels. Where do they get all their ambition?

JANET
(*quietly*) I don't think that's possible.

ARTHUR
What isn't?

JANET
(*coming out of a daydream*) What did I just say?

ARTHUR
No idea.

JANET
I think I was asleep.

ARTHUR
Are you sure there was no note?

JANET
Why would she leave a note when she would rather leave us all in a state of whatever this state is she's left us in?

ARTHUR
I never in a million years thought she'd go through with her plan.

JANET
Well, she hasn't quite gone through with it, has she?

ARTHUR
What are they saying?

JANET
You were right there in the ER.

ARTHUR
I wasn't listening. I've never liked emergency waiting rooms.

JANET
I don't think you're supposed to like them. They were saying that if she has ruptured anything, they won't know until they do the CT scan tomorrow. It's hard to tell with the brain, especially Marion's.

ARTHUR
Why would he be just sitting there?

JANET
(*suddenly more present*) Is he back?

ARTHUR
Who?

JANET
Mr. Bodmer?

ARTHUR
No. That squirrel, sitting there, looking up at the house. Why?

JANET
How should I know? Go ask him.

ARTHUR
Every other squirrel is running around doing squirrel things,
but he just sits there, studying us through the window. Still
wondering about Mr. Bodmer?

JANET
I was just –

ARTHUR
What?

JANET
I didn't like their line of questioning, those ambulance people.
Asking about pills. As if we were aware of every single item on
every single bathroom shelf.

ARTHUR
I don't think they were insinuating anything.

JANET
Then why did they keep asking?

ARTHUR
It's their job. You should never have told them about her
birthday plan.

JANET
I was nervous.

ARTHUR
Poor Marion.

JANET
Let's not have any "poor Marion," please. For the rest of
our days, it'll be "poor Marion." How about "poor Janet"?
Lived in a house with her gay husband and not-so-gay sister.
Found in her dusty attic, surrounded by boxes and boxes of
unrealized potential.

ARTHUR
Ex-husband.

JANET
Ex nothing. You're still here. We're both still here.

JANET's mind drifts away once again.

ARTHUR
This is not a good time to have a discussion about lost potential.
Your sister is in the hospital. She may never be the same.
Although that might be –

JANET
She'll be the same. We'll all be the same.

*At last ARTHUR turns away from the window to
announce something.*

ARTHUR
I don't think I'm gay, Janet.

JANET
And just when I don't care. Your timing is impeccable.

ARTHUR
I was, you know. I really was. And then I wasn't. I don't know
what I mean.

JANET
But you do know what you mean. You mean it was high time to
move on, from this, from us, and it was.

ARTHUR
I want to come back to you.

JANET
Come back? You haven't even moved your nose-hair trimmer
from my bathroom vanity.

ARTHUR
I've always considered that *our* bathroom vanity.

JANET
Arthur, you slept with a pediatrician who ran off with a dog walker. I'm willing to forgive a lot of things, even that, but I cannot accept being just some fallen ... petal in the ... wilting flower of your ... senectitude.

ARTHUR
I don't think that's a terribly good analogy.

JANET
The time has passed for terribly good analogies.

ARTHUR
I have lived nearly my entire life without knowing why. The only thing that makes even the slightest sense is being here, in this house, with you.

JANET
My bags are packed.

ARTHUR
They are?

JANET
In my mind, Arthur, in my mind they're waiting at the door. Don't look at the door. I said "in my mind."

ARTHUR
Where would we go?

JANET
Not we, me. We?

ARTHUR
And what about me?

JANET
You're an adult, you can go wherever you like.

ARTHUR
I don't want to go wherever I like. I tried that. I'll go wherever *you* like. It's so much better for me.

JANET
Arthur, if you've lived your entire life without knowing why, isn't it time you found out?

JANET gets up and leaves. ARTHUR collapses into a chair.

Blackout.

SCENE 4

It's the middle of the night. Only lamplight from the street shines, grimly, through the window. There is a pronounced knock at the door. After a long beat, a light goes on in the hallway. JANET walks through in her robe. We hear –

JANET
Hello. Who is it?

Beat.

Who is it?

We hear the door open a little, then a little more.

Hello?

Nothing. She shuts the door again and locks it. She walks into the living room. She goes to the window and looks out. ARTHUR appears in his pyjamas, half-awake.

ARTHUR
Who was it?

JANET steps away from the window, wondering.

JANET
No one.

Blackout.

SCENE FIVE

Afternoon. MARION is seated in her usual place. Her hair is a bit different, any makeup she was wearing is gone, but she's reading the same book. We hear sounds at the door. JANET enters in coat, carrying a shopping bag; we hear her shivering.

JANET
What on earth is happening in the park?

MARION says nothing.

JANET
It's all blocked off with police cars. (*noticing MARION*) You haven't moved.

MARION
I have.

JANET
The agent is coming in about five minutes. This room is a mess.

MARION
People buy houses, not the mess that's in them.

JANET
Are you going to look at that apartment today?

MARION
I don't like where it is.

JANET
What about that other one, with the French doors?

MARION
French *door*. There's only one. And I'm not convinced of its nationality.

JANET
You're running out of options.

MARION
I'm thinking of moving to Italy.

JANET
Marion, you need to get serious about this.

MARION
I don't know why you're so concerned. I can take care of myself.

JANET
You can?

MARION
Has it occurred to you, Janet, that the reason I never do
anything is because you do everything for me? You always have.

JANET
And who else would?

MARION
What are you afraid of, exactly? That I won't make
it on my own?

JANET
You did try to kill yourself.

MARION
And I didn't succeed. Perhaps you should have more faith in my
inabilities.

JANET
You did succeed. Arthur and I were going out the next night.
You could have done it then. You would have been dead by the
time we got home. But here you are.

MARION
Here I am.

JANET
Not for long, because I'm selling the house. I don't care if you
kill yourself, if that's what you want. But that's not what you
want. You want everything to stay the same.

MARION
So do you.

JANET
Are you kidding me? You're kidding me.

MARION
You thrive on unhappiness. You lash out at the world and
pretend to be angry, but it's just an act. You like things the way
they are. If you ever did go to Mexico – which is unlikely since
you don't even like enchiladas – you'd go insane. The toilet
situation alone.

JANET
You think I'm happy here?

MARION
You don't *want* to be happy. If you did, you would never have
married Arthur.

JANET
And what do I want?

MARION
To avoid the terrible truth that our lives are slowly killing us.

JANET
A little too slowly.

MARION shrugs pointedly, heading to the window.

MARION
They found a dead man, by the way – since you asked.

JANET
Who did?

MARION
The police. That's what they're doing out there. They found a
dead man in the park. It's why you had to go around.

JANET
You're making this up.

MARION
I'm not.

JANET
Dead? Where?

MARION
The whippet sniffed him out. He was in a recycling bin, which if
you're a Buddhist, I suppose, is reassuring.

JANET
Who was he?

MARION
Must've been someone.

JANET
Dead?

MARION
A murder in the park, by the way, isn't going to do much for
property values.

   MARION exits. Blackout.

SCENE SIX

Later. ARTHUR is seated, perusing a laptop on the sofa.
JANET looks out the window.

ARTHUR
  What did she say about the roof?

JANET
  Do you think I thrive on unhappiness?

ARTHUR
  No. Yes. What's that got to do with the roof?

JANET
  She said we should fix it.

ARTHUR
  What's the point if we're selling?

JANET
  It's a material fact that must be disclosed. And we can't just add
  it to the price. I's simpler, she said, and cheaper for it not to be a
  part of the negotiation.

ARTHUR
  And how much is her commission?

JANET
  You heard about the dead man.

ARTHUR
  Dead man?

JANET
  They found a dead man in the big recycling bin behind
  the washrooms.

ARTHUR
Where?

JANET
Behind the washrooms.

ARTHUR
Murder?

JANET
Well, you don't get into one of those things by accident.

ARTHUR
Who was he?

JANET
I went over to have a look. They've cordoned off the whole area
with yellow tape. There was an officer taking pictures.

Beat.

Five percent.

ARTHUR
What?

JANET
Split between the two agents.

ARTHUR
There are two?

JANET
It's all there. Look for yourself. She says the park will sell
the house. The park is "the soul of the neighbourhood," she
says. Who knew the soul had a filthy public washroom with
seatless toilets?

ARTHUR
I'm terrible at reading this stuff. A dead man? In the
recycling bin?

JANET
Just sign the thing.

ARTHUR
I can't. This is our house. This is our life.

JANET
(*after a considered beat*) You know, Arthur, I think I knew you
were gay when I married you.

ARTHUR
I told you, I'm not gay.

JANET
Why don't you let others be the judge of that?

ARTHUR
I don't know what I was.

JANET
Arthur, you found something out about yourself – that you're
not who you thought you were. Gay or not gay, it doesn't matter.
I think you're right. I wanted to control your life. I wanted to
make you into something you could never be.

ARTHUR
It doesn't matter.

JANET
Of course it matters.

ARTHUR
There's only one thing that counts.

JANET
Don't say "love."

ARTHUR
Love. I want to be with you.

JANET
Oh, Arthur. I can't just sit here and watch my life drift past.
Well, anyway, I won't be able to.

ARTHUR
The operation –

JANET
The doctor – he said the operation – I'm not having
the operation.

ARTHUR
Why not?

JANET
It's risky, and it might not work. I'm done with all the futility.

ARTHUR
Let's go blind together. Let's grow lame and senile and infirm.
Let's never look back. Or let's only look back. Let's measure out
our life in sugar spoons.

JANET
I think you're confusing T.S. Eliot with Mary Poppins.

ARTHUR
Yes, let's do that. Let's confuse things. Who's going to stop us?

JANET
No one.

ARTHUR
I'm too old to be gay *or* straight. And you're too old to care.
Only one thing matters, now.

JANET
(*escaping the room*) Don't say love.

Blackout.

SCENE SEVEN

Afternoon. ARTHUR pockets his phone and looks out the
window as MARION enters and pours herself a drink.
ARTHUR sits, thinking.

ARTHUR
He called from Arizona.

MARION
Your little man?

ARTHUR
Yes.

MARION
Was it a short conversation?

ARTHUR
His dog walker found another dog walker. My "little man"
wants me back.

MARION
So, what are you waiting for?

ARTHUR
What am I waiting for? (*shifting gears*) Her eye news wasn't
good. Did she tell you?

MARION
Never trust an ophthalmologist.

ARTHUR
Poor thing.

MARION
She'll be all right.

ARTHUR
And completely blind within the year.

MARION
She'll see things she couldn't have seen.

ARTHUR
And be more miserable than she's ever been.

MARION
What if she's happier? What if we're all happier? At least she's
taken the house off the market.

ARTHUR
Her last stand.

MARION
Withrow Park.

ARTHUR
What are they measuring now?

MARION
I don't think Janet will get an answer out of that officer.

ARTHUR
Why not?

MARION
He's parking enforcement.

MARION walks away and sits.

ARTHUR
I'm not even curious, frankly.

MARION
It's our mystery man. I know it is.

ARTHUR
Mystery man?

MARION
The one who never showed up for dinner, obviously.

ARTHUR
There are other reasons people don't show up for dinner besides being murdered.

MARION
Yes, but it's a very good excuse.

ARTHUR
There's eye surgery – something to do with drainage canals – but she doesn't want it.

MARION
And I agreed with her. Too risky. Sometimes we just need to accept our fate, Arthur.

ARTHUR
Is that what you did?

MARION
It's what I'm doing now. I had a very strange dream in the hospital. The mystery man from the park came for dinner after all. He told us an unbelievable story and we were quite enthralled.

   Beat.

ARTHUR
What was the story?

MARION
I have no idea, but it was unbelievable.

ARTHUR
How do you know it was if you don't know what it was?

MARION
I remember that it was. Dreams don't have dramatic structure,
Arthur. You never should've taught English.

ARTHUR
Social studies, but do go on.

MARION
I woke up and I thought, "What if I'm still dreaming? What if
I've killed myself?"

ARTHUR
If you'd killed yourself, you wouldn't be dreaming.

MARION
We don't have to be the same person, Arthur. We can wake up
and be someone else.

ARTHUR
Can we?

MARION
I decided, when I came to, Janet will need someone. When she
loses her sight, I'll be called to action.

ARTHUR
Janet's always been the guide. I had this romantic notion of
being her eyes, her sight, her window to the world, which has
somehow evaporated.

MARION
Audio description isn't for everyone.

ARTHUR
(as if quoting) We're never quite as good as our intentions.

MARION.
Who said that?

ARTHUR
I did. I'm not sure what I'm capable of.

MARION
Leaving, I hope. The last thing a blind person needs is one more
object to trip over.

MARION and ARTHUR watch Janet from the window.

ARTHUR
Look at her. Just swinging on the swing. All alone.

MARION
We would have made an interesting couple.

ARTHUR
Really?

MARION
But I had to let you go.

ARTHUR
Oh, you let me go.

MARION
Not very far.

Beat.

I could've taken you places you never went with her.

ARTHUR
What exactly are you talking about?

MARION looks at him, then back out the window.

MARION
My life changed forever that day on the beach.

ARTHUR
What day?

MARION
A day you don't remember that I will never forget. You asked me about Janet. It was our first time together, our first date, and yet you asked me about Janet. I should've known then that I didn't exist for you. But I was foolish enough to fall in love anyway. Janet, of course, couldn't care less about you. It took some persuading on my part for her to change her mind. Imagine us, now, living together in this house, you and me.

ARTHUR
We do.

MARION
And Janet, the sister-in-law. You might not be running off with a tiny little pediatrician, and Janet might have followed her heart. Don't ever tell her.

ARTHUR
No.

MARION
Nobody ever lives their real lives.

ARTHUR
Then whose are these?

Blackout.

SCENE EIGHT

From out of the darkness, SIMON appears, his naked body marked for post-mortem incisions.

SIMON

Whose lives these? This flesh, this blood? This makeshift vessel that transports us from one side to the other, this body, these limbs, only to disintegrate. And what remains a study, as you can see. Forgive my appearance, but it's an autopsy and who am I to argue? They'll cut me open and have a good look, they'll take out all the parts and weigh them and put them in plastic bags and put it all back inside. And they will come no closer to understanding me. How I died, yes, but not how I lived. Sleeping under your eaves, warmed only by the thought of your comfort. After they've done with all of this, they'll burn it and it will all go up in smoke, but don't worry, I'm not going to leave you. I'm right here in the park. No, I'm not an angel. I'm not looking out for you, only looking in.

SIMON blows into the air. Blackout.

SCENE NINE

JANET walks across the room, eyes closed. She stops, opens them.

JANET

Right. Eight steps to the middle of nowhere.

JANET closes her eyes again, counting steps to Marion's chair until she comes across Marion's novel. JANET opens her eyes. MARION enters from the kitchen in a coat, with a shopping bag.

MARION

I'm off to get fish!

JANET

Somebody really should read this thing one day.

MARION

And spoil the suspense?

JANET makes her way to the window and closes her eyes.

MARION

How's the practice?

JANET

The light. I can find the window even with my eyes closed.

JANET opens her eyes. MARION joins JANET at the window.

MARION

They've removed the yellow tape. He was a younger man, apparently. Homeless.

JANET

Who told you that?

MARION
  It's amazing what you can get out of the police by supplying them with the wrong information.

JANET
  Do you think –

MARION
  Think? I knew it all along.

JANET
  Oh God, it makes sense! He never showed that night.

MARION
  They're going to install cameras in the park.

JANET
  Mr. Bodmer.

> *Beat. JANET and MARION continue looking out the window.*

MARION
  Stupid woman. Just keeps talking on that phone. After all that's happened. Her dog is pooing in the sandbox.

JANET
  The things I won't miss seeing.

MARION
  Now that he's sniffed out the dead body, I suppose he feels somewhat vindicated. Managed to expose us all.

JANET
  From Eden banished and our sins laid bare.

MARION
  Look. A new mailman. Oh. He smiled at me. Why?

JANET
You're so odd with men.

MARION
Me?

JANET
You were very odd with Arthur, remember? When we
first met him?

MARION
Was I?

JANET
You went out with him, and then suddenly, that was it. Over.
And I got stuck with him.

MARION
Why did you ever marry him in the first place? I know it's a bit
late to ask, but timing isn't everything.

JANET
Why does anybody do anything? Have you never offered
someone the seat next to you on the streetcar suspecting there's
worse to come? Better occupied than take your chances, she
said, summing up her life.

MARION
No one sits next to me on the streetcar. It's surprising what a
toothy grin can do. I'm off. (*looking out the window, excited*)
Look. He's gone.

JANET
Who?

MARION
The whippet. Look. Leash and all. Furiously chasing something.
(*as she goes*) God only knows what.

JANET
Bring an umbrella, otherwise it'll surely rain.

MARION leaves. JANET resumes her practice, closing her eyes and touching something invisible.

JANET
Simon?

JANET opens her eyes. No one.

SCENE TEN

*The lights change and time passes, but JANET remains at
the window. As the lights come up, ARTHUR enters the hall
with a suitcase, frantic.*

ARTHUR
Has anyone seen my raincoat?

JANET
Marion is fixing lunch.

ARTHUR
I'm not staying. I've called the taxi.

JANET
Playground. Fountain.

ARTHUR
You're making me do this. You're making me leave.

JANET
You won't need a raincoat in Arizona.

ARTHUR
What are you looking at?

JANET
While I can still see things, I'm committing them all to memory.

ARTHUR
Janet.

JANET
I'm not making you do anything you don't want to do. And
feeling guilty is no reason to stay. Marion will look after me.

ARTHUR
Marion can't look after herself.

JANET
We've all been in a trance. It's time to wake up, fingers snapped.

ARTHUR
What will we wake up to? That is the question?

JANET continues looking.

ARTHUR
I'm not going to Arizona.

JANET
A new development.

ARTHUR
I've ended it. Well, it was already ended. I'm heading off by myself. I don't know what I was thinking.

JANET
You weren't thinking, you were feeling. It doesn't matter what.

ARTHUR
Would you like to know where I'm headed?

JANET
Well, I suppose you'll tell me.

ARTHUR
I'll tell you. Farther south.

JANET
South.

ARTHUR
You'll laugh.

JANET
No. I won't.

ARTHUR
You'll laugh.

JANET
I won't.

ARTHUR
Machu Picchu. You're laughing.

JANET
I'm not even smiling.

ARTHUR
Inside.

JANET
Well. Yes, inside. But I'm smiling because you might finally catch up with yourself there. And, of course, because I was right all along.

ARTHUR
No wonder I let you run my life. You're so much better at it than I ever was.

JANET
I love you, Arthur.

JANET kisses ARTHUR's forehead.

Please don't say you'll come back.

ARTHUR
I'll come back.

MARION enters with lunch things.

MARION
Lunch!

JANET
He can't find his raincoat.

MARION
You won't need a raincoat in Arizona.

ARTHUR
No.

MARION
Grilled cheese.

JANET
Get out while you can.

ARTHUR
The taxi's coming.

MARION
Taxi?

JANET
(*to ARTHUR*) Passport?

ARTHUR suddenly rushes out to the hallway.

ARTHUR
My passport!

JANET
It's in his pocket.

MARION puts down the lunch things, somewhat devastated.

JANET
Just us.

MARION
Just us.

ARTHUR returns back, breathless.

ARTHUR
It was right here in my pocket.

MARION
What are the chances?

ARTHUR
I can't – stay. I – goodbye.

ARTHUR goes to JANET and kisses her on the cheek.

Goodbye, Janet. I love you.

*JANET pats him on the arm, affectionately. He goes to
MARION and takes her hand in his.*

MARION
Arthur –

ARTHUR
Goodbye, Marion.

MARION cries without making a sound. ARTHUR holds her.

JANET
We're all on a journey, now. To the desert, but not to the desert.
To the moon, and who knows where. Beyond. To no place.

A car horn sounds. ARTHUR breaks free.

Then one evening right down Logan Avenue, heaven will lay
itself down for us, and up we'll go, if the wind is right, swing up,
and into the night sky.

ARTHUR picks up his suitcase.

ARTHUR
I –

JANET
I don't believe in any of it, of course, but what does that matter?

Another car horn outside. ARTHUR exits.

JANET
Believe or don't believe, the stars are waiting. Time
has found us.

The door shuts behind ARTHUR.

But there's a little bit of road ahead. A bit of road.

MARION sits.

A bit more suffering and solitude, and memories like fireflies,
quick to come and go, and truth and deception. Journeys
that go nowhere, and quiet days, a few more anyway, filled
with adventure.

MARION
And grilled cheese, although I forgot the cheese. Sorry.

JANET
And afternoon tea.

MARION
And afternoon gin.

JANET
Yes. And Christmas soon enough.

MARION
Christmas! Oh, God. Another Christmas.

JANET
Easter. Thanksgiving.

MARION
And shopping.

JANET
Yes. And tired, swollen feet. And one last laugh.

MARION
We can only hope. And unfriendly fish, don't forget.

JANET
Who could forget? And basmati rice and stolen umbrellas. And one more surprise. And one last disappointment.

MARION
For certain.

JANET
Are you crying? What are you crying about, for heaven's sake?

MARION
Nothing.

JANET
Nothing. Look at the sun through the trees, Marion; so many colours.

MARION joins JANET at the window.

Is that a man, sitting over on the bench?

MARION
No. Just the light, spying in on us.

JANET
The light. Lower and lower.

MARION
Winter coming.

JANET
Then spring.

MARION
So it begins. The end of our days.

JANET
And off we go.

As they gaze out into the park, the lights fade.

Originally from Calgary, Alberta, **Morris Panych** is arguably Canada's most celebrated playwright and director. His plays have garnered countless awards including two Governor General's Literary Awards for Drama (for *The Ends of the Earth* and *Girl in the Goldfish Bowl*), fourteen Jessie Richardson Awards (Vancouver), and five Dora Mavor Moore Awards (Toronto). Productions of the much-lauded *Vigil*, *Girl in the Goldfish Bowl*, *Gordon*, *The Trespassers*, and *Lawrence & Holloman* have been mounted in Canada, the United States, Europe, Asia, Australia, and New Zealand. His plays have been produced in over two dozen languages. He has written twenty-five works for the stage and has directed over a hundred productions across Canada and the United States, including operas and dance.

Mr. Panych makes his home in Toronto. kenandmorris.com.